THE FRENCH REVOLUTION

Martin Dickinson

Deputy Head, Hinchingbrooke School, Huntingdon

Nelson

For James and Matthew

Thomas Nelson and Sons Ltd
Nelson House Mayfield Road
Walton-on-Thames Surrey
KT12 5PL UK

Nelson Blackie
Wester Cleddens Road
Bishopbriggs
Glasgow
G64 2NZ UK

Thomas Nelson Australia
102 Dodds Street
South Melbourne
Victoria 3205 Australia

Nelson Canada
1120 Birchmount Road
Scarborough Ontario
M1K 5G4 Canada

First published by Macmillan Education Ltd 1984
(under ISBN 0-333-35076-6)

This edition published by Thomas Nelson and Sons Ltd 1992

I(T)P Thomas Nelson is an International
       Thomson Publishing Company

I(T)P is used under licence

ISBN 0-17-435079-1
NPN 9 8 7 6 5

Printed in China

Author's Acknowledgement
Numerous people have helped with this book but I would
especially like to thank John Shearring from Sir Henry Cooper
High School, Hull, for help with some of the assignments and
Susan, my wife, who checked and typed the manuscript.

CONTENTS

Acknowledgements

The author and publishers wish to thank the following who have kindly given permission for the use of copyright material:

Basil Blackwell Publisher Limited for extracts from *French Revolution Documents* by J M Roberts, *The French Revolution* by J M Thompson and *Leaders of the French Revolution* by J M Thompson; J M Dent & Sons Ltd. for an extract from *Travels in France and Italy During the Years 1787–89* (Everyman's Library); Mrs Ida Gershoy for an extract from *The Era of the French Revolution* by L Gershoy published by Wadsworth Publishing Company; Heinemann Educational Books for an extract from *Heinemann English Dictionary* by Harber & Payton; Longman Group Limited for extracts from *Revolution and Terror in France 1789–95* by D G Wright; Oxford University Press for extracts from *Reactions to the French Revolution* by Richard Cobb (1972), and an extract from *The Concise Oxford Dictionary*, 7th Edition, 1982; Past and Present Society for extracts from the article 'Women in Revolution 1789–1796' by Olwen Hufton, from *Past and Present*, No. 53, November 1971; Penguin Books Ltd. for an extract from Alfred Cobban's *A History of Modern France*, Vol. 1. (Pelican Books, Third Edition 1963) Copyright © the Estate of Alfred Cobban; Routledge and Kegan Paul Ltd. for an extract from *A Social History of the French Revolution* by Norman Hampson; Martin Secker & Warburg Ltd. for extracts from *The French Revolution* by Pernoud and Flaissier; Times Newspapers Limited for an extract from *The Times Reports: The French Revolution* by N Ascherson.

The author and publishers wish to acknowledge, with thanks, the following photographic sources:

BBC Hulton Picture Library p. 43 bottom; Bibliotheque Nationale, Paris pp. 11, 32, 37; Bulloz pp. 5, 13 left, 17, 35, 43 top, 45; Fotomas Index pp. 24, 27; Giraudon pp. 29, 36 top; Mansell Collection pp. 6, 13 right, 15, 16, 18, 22, 23, 30, 34, 36 bottom; Musée Cambinet p. 47; Musée Carnavalet/Bulloz pp. 40, 44; Oxfam p. 38; Popperfoto p. 46; H. Roger Viollet pp. 8, 10, 21, 41; Snark International p. 26.

The publishers have made every effort to trace the copyright holders, but if they have inadvertently overlooked any, they will be pleased to make the necessary arrangements at the first opportunity.

PREFACE

The study of history is exciting, whether in a good story well told, a mystery solved by the judicious unravelling of clues, or a study of the men, women and children, whose fears and ambitions, successes and tragedies make up the collective memory of mankind.

This series aims to reveal this excitement to pupils through a set of topic books on important historical subjects from the Middle Ages to the present day. Each book contains four main elements: a narrative and descriptive text, lively and relevant illustrations, extracts of contemporary evidence, and questions for further thought and work. Involvement in these elements should provide an adventure which will bring the past to life in the imagination of the pupil.

Each book is also designed to develop the knowledge, skills and concepts so essential to a pupil's growth. It provides a wide, varying introduction to the evidence available on each topic. In handling this evidence, pupils will increase their understanding of basic historical concepts like causation and change, as well as of more advanced ideas like revolution and democracy. In addition, their use of basic study skills will be complemented by more sophisticated historical skills such as the detection of bias and the formulation of opinion.

The intended audience for the series is pupils of eleven to sixteen years: it is expected that the earlier topics will be in introduced in the first three years of secondary school, while the nineteenth and twentieth century topics are directed towards first examinations.

The execution of King Louis XVI, 21 January 1793

1 INTRODUCTION

The execution of King Louis XVI

Early in the morning of Tuesday 21 January 1793, Louis XVI of France was woken by his guards for the last time. He had been imprisoned together with his wife, Queen Marie-Antoinette, his wife's sister and his two children since the previous August. Now he was to die.

He was allowed to receive Mass and at about 8.30 a.m. he left in the mayor's closed carriage. It was a cold, misty morning. Troops formed a convoy around the carriage and National Guardsmen lined the four-kilometre route to the Place de la Revolution. Those in charge of the day's proceedings feared a possible rescue attempt by supporters

National Guard: a kind of citizens' police force established in 1789

of the king and they were taking no chances. Drums beat all the time but the people lining the streets were silent.

The journey took about an hour. A huge crowd had gathered in the Place de la Revolution and large numbers of troops surrounded the scaffold. After mounting the scaffold with his priest, Louis removed his coat and cravat and unfastened his shirt collar. His arms were tied and his hair was cut with a large pair of scissors by one of the executioners. Appearing somewhat upset at these actions Louis then signalled that he wished to speak to the crowd. The drums ceased and Louis started: 'My people, I die an innocent man.' He clearly wished to continue but the drums started up again and drowned his words. The two executioners seized him and placed him on the guillotine. A moment later his severed head was held up to the crowd.

It was greeted with cheers. People threw their hats into the air, danced around the guillotine and dipped handkerchiefs or scraps of paper in the king's blood. Some tried to seize the body but this was hastily taken away by guards and buried, together with the severed head, in a grave dug three metres deep. The official time of death was 10.22 a.m.

Louis XVI. King of France 1774–1792. Before the Revolution the king alone had the right to rule and traditionally this right was seen as coming from God. The king was God's representative. Hence the title: 'Louis, by the Grace of God, King of France.'

The French Revolution: a time of change

The execution of King Louis XVI shows very dramatically how much France had changed as a result of the French Revolution. Throughout the eighteenth century the king of France was regarded as one of the most powerful monarchs in Europe. Yet here he was being taken through the streets of Paris like a criminal and guillotined in front of his people. It was a decisive break with the past. As you will see, events in France between 1789 and 1794 brought many important and permanent changes to that country. Moreover, the impact of the Revolution spread beyond France and continued to be felt long after 1794. Many of the ideas it developed are still very much with us today. Of course not everything changed. France is a very large country (over twice the size of Great Britain) and those who lived in the many isolated villages and small towns were often cut off from events in Paris. Nevertheless, things could never be the same after the Revolution.

In some ways it might be more accurate to talk about the French Revolutions rather than *the* French Revolution. Many people, for many different reasons, were discontented in France on the eve of the Revolution. What gave the Revolution its impact was that a number of different crises came to a head at the same time. Imagine a series of powder kegs joined by fuses; set a match to one and before long they will all explode. In a sense this is what happened in France between 1789 and 1794.

2

FRANCE BEFORE THE REVOLUTION

An incident in Paris

Richard Cobb recounts the following episode in his book *Reactions to the French Revolution*:

Champs-Elysées: a main street in Paris
Bourguignon: a man from Burgundy in central eastern France
livery: special clothes worn by the servants of a particular family
maréchaussée: mounted police
commissaire: police commissioner
les Grands: 'The Great Ones', i.e. the wealthiest and most powerful noble families

When first in Paris, in 1759, as a young printer's apprentice, Restif goes for a walk, with a girl on his arm, along the still untended, semi-wild avenues off the Champs-Elysées. After a time, he is caught up with by two elegant young men in silk jackets and carrying swords, who begin to walk at the same level as the couple, stopping when they do, keeping pace with them, jostling the young man and his girl, closing in more and more on Restif, persistently jogging his arm, tripping him with their feet, to the insistent accompaniment of the phrase: 'What will it take to annoy him?' The young Bourguignon looks stolidly ahead, refusing to be provoked. After a few more yards of this scene, with the four still walking abreast, one of the young men, after placing his swagger stick in some dirt on the road, holds it up to Restif's nose: 'Will this annoy him?' Restif has had enough; breaking away from the girl, he picks up a piece of building material – a plank or a long piece of wood, lying by the path – and sets about the pair with it, to such effect that his aggressors, after a thorough trouncing, take to their heels. But the scene has been observed, and, immediately, the apprentice is set upon by a group of servants in livery. At the same time, a horseman of the maréchaussée, *riding by, pulls in his horse. The two young men, returning to the scene, ask him to take Restif in charge. He is soon brought before the* commissaire *of Chaillot and is about to be confined, before appearing in front of a magistrate, when the poor girl breaks down and starts weeping. The young men, perhaps moved, and anxious to make at least a token display of gallantry, tell the* commissaire *that the whole thing had been a joke and that they wish to withdraw the charge; they then take their leave, followed by the servants. The* commissaire *tells Restif that he had been fortunate, asking at the same time if he had recognised the livery of the servants; the apprentice, a newcomer to the capital, states that he has not. 'It is the livery of the Duke of Orleans', comments the* commissaire. *Restif was to recall the incident in 1784, when he was writing that section of* Monsieur Nicolas *that dealt with his early life in Paris. 'Such is the tyranny of les Grands', he then observes.*

Questions
1 How would Restif know that the men pestering him were wealthy before he discovered who they were?
2 Had the case gone ahead, what do you think Restif might have said in his defence?
3 What does this story tell us about the young noblemen's attitude towards Restif?
4 What do you think Restif meant by his remark 'Such is the tyranny of *les Grands*'?

The nobility

It so happened that Restif raised his stick against two members of one of the richest and most powerful families in France. Only a few hundred noble families were known as *les Grands*. They owned huge estates, held the most important jobs and dominated the royal court at Versailles. Altogether there were about 400 000 men, women and children of noble birth in France in 1789; far more than in England, for example. Not all, however, were wealthy. Arthur Young, the Englishman who travelled through France on the eve of the Revolution, met some 'so poor that they plough their own fields'.

Marie-Antoinette at Versailles, 1775. Below right: the royal court in 1771

The Church

Many of the best positions reserved for the nobility were in the Church. Indeed by 1789 all bishops in France were of noble birth. Bishops, like abbots of monasteries and other high-ranking Church figures, were extremely wealthy. Some of them were also clearly more interested in winning the king's favour at Versailles than in devoting their lives to God. For example, in 1787 the Archbishop of Toulouse became the king's chief minister.

The majority of the 100 000 clergy, however, were village priests who lived in poverty and understood only too well the problems faced by the peasant families who made up their congregations. In general those who lived in the country were devout Catholics and the priest was a respected and influential figure. He might well be the only person in the village who could read or write.

Privilege

The Church owned about a tenth of all land in France and the rents from this brought in vast revenues. It was not, however, compelled to pay any taxes. Anything the government received from the Church was donated by the clergy as a 'free gift' and represented only a small fraction of the Church's annual income. In this sense the Church was privileged and privileges of one kind or another were extremely common in eighteenth-century France. As noblemen, the two men who pestered Restif and his girl had the right to wear swords. They were also exempted from paying certain taxes. Financial privileges, however, were not confined to the clergy and the nobility. Certain provinces, for example, traditionally had a lighter tax burden. In this case the privilege extended to all those who paid taxes within the province.

Finance

This mass of financial privileges caused great problems for the government, which as the years went by became increasingly short of money. The difficulty was that nobody wished to surrender these privileges, least of all the clergy and the nobility. At the same time the government was spending heavily, especially on war. France was at war, chiefly with Britain, for forty-one years during the period 1688–1783. In order to survive, the government borrowed heavily and in this way vast debts were accumulated.

The War of American Independence, in which France supported the American colonists against Britain from 1778 to 1783, crippled France financially. Financiers became increasingly reluctant to lend money to the government and so in 1786 Calonne, the king's finance minister, proposed a new land tax to which there would be no exemptions. This would have reduced the financial privileges of the clergy and nobility and not surprisingly these groups did their best to oppose it. In the face of their opposition (sometimes called the Revolt of the Nobility) the king was forced to back down.

So by 1788 France was bankrupt, and in desperation Louis agreed to the summoning of the States General. This was an elected assembly (roughly equivalent to the British Houses of Parliament), which had not met since 1614. Louis hoped that it might find some way of solving the country's financial problems. In fact once the States General met in May 1789 events rapidly passed out of his control. The French Revolution had begun.

The middle classes

A prisoner is broken on the wheel. Savage punishments like this were still carried out in the eighteenth century

The eruption happened in this way because some people, including many of the elected delegates, hoped that the States General would try to change France very considerably indeed. These were the middle classes, well-educated people such as lawyers or lower government officials whose careers were blocked by their lack of a noble title. They felt they should have a say in the running of the country and wanted the king to hand over many of his powers to an elected assembly. They argued that everyone should have certain basic rights. These included the right to be free from the horrors of the torture chamber and the right to be brought to trial if arrested. These rights did not exist in eighteenth-century France. For example, anybody could be imprisoned without trial if the king chose to issue a special order called a *lettre de cachet*:

> *Take the road to Lourde, where is a castle on a rock, garrisoned for the mere purpose of keeping state prisoners, sent hither by* lettres de cachet.
>
> Arthur Young, an Englishman, writing in 1787

Paris

After July 1788, when the king announced the summoning of the States General, there was a widespread feeling that important changes were on the way. This expectant mood affected country as well as town because all villages were asked to state their grievances. In Paris the excitement reached fever pitch. Political clubs were formed, pamphlets were published in profusion and coffee houses were filled to overflowing with people listening to anybody prepared to climb on to their table or chair and address the assembled customers.

All this activity took place at a time when the ordinary people of Paris were becoming increasingly short of food. Out of the city's population of well over half a million, perhaps 80 000 were unemployed. During the summer of 1788 the harvest in the Paris region was destroyed by a freak hailstorm (there were reports of hailstones 'sixteen inches in circumference'). The winter which followed was exceptionally harsh and as a result many thousands of people had

Food shortages were not new. This picture is dated 1693. What do you think is happening?

flocked to Paris from the surrounding villages in search of food. With food in short supply, prices rose dramatically from 9 *sous* for a 4 lb loaf to 14½ *sous* by February 1789, so that a typical worker was now spending three-quarters of his wages on bread. Bread queues lengthened and tension mounted. One newspaper wrote:

> *Each baker's shop was surrounded by a crowd that received a very mean ration and the next day's supply was never sure. The complaints of those who had queued all day without getting anything increased the alarm of the rest. There were frequent fights for bread.*

In April and May 1789 two men and a woman were hanged and five others were branded with hot irons and sent to the galleys after serious food riots in the east of the city. An explosive situation was developing in the capital.

The complaints of the peasants

The majority of people in eighteenth-century France (perhaps 22 million out of a population of about 26 million in 1789) were peasants. For the most part they eked out a miserable existence on the land. They farmed inefficiently and a run of bad harvests could send them roaming the countryside in search of food. A substantial increase in population during the eighteenth century had made things worse. (Estimates of the country's population in 1715 vary between 17 and 20 million.) There were more people wanting their share of the available land and so peasant holdings diminished in size until many of them were not large enough to support a family. Food was becoming more expensive to buy and yet all the time there were more mouths to feed. 'The number of our children reduces us to desperation,' complained some peasants.

The peasants had many complaints on the eve of the Revolution. One way of looking at them a little more closely is by studying the *cahiers de doléances*, or lists of grievances, which were produced throughout France in 1788–89. This was done on the king's command as part of the preparations for the meeting of the States General. Every village drew up its *cahier*. Here is part of the one drawn up by the Parish of Longnes:

A   *1*   *We beg His Majesty to abolish all the* gabelles...

       2   *We wish His Majesty to abolish all the unfair taxes which have been placed on daily necessities such as food...*

       4   *We wish His Majesty to ensure that the* tailles *and other taxes we pay for the upkeep of the State are imposed on all castles, houses, cultivated lands, meadows, woods, vineyards, moors, ponds and rivers, indeed on everything...*

gabelle: tax on salt
taille: the main tax collected by the government. It might take half the value of a peasant's harvest.

11

feudal dues: point 8 of the cahier is referring to one of a number of obligations or dues imposed on many peasants by the local *seigneur* or lord of the manor. His charges were high and these dues were bitterly resented.

5 *We wish to make known the burden involved in building a road which will only be used by some lord travelling to his castle.*

7 *We beg His Majesty to permit us to kill rabbits and pigeons which are too numerous and which cause considerable damage in the countryside.*

8 *We want the obligation to use the lord's mill abolished...*

9 *We want horse thieves and those who steal other animals dealt with according to the law.*

These grievances are listed in the presence of most of the inhabitants of Longnes this eighth day of March 1789.

J.M. Roberts: *French Revolution Documents* (i), 1966

Questions

1 Points 1, 2 and 4 all ask for the abolition of certain taxes. What do these taxes have in common? How might this help to explain why people felt so strongly about them?
2 What evidence is there about the attitude of the people of this village towards the wealthy?
3 Point 7 gives one reason why these people wished to be allowed to kill game. Can you suggest another?
4 What conclusions do you draw from point 9?

B Another source of evidence about peasant life is the diary kept by the Englishman Arthur Young as he travelled through France during the years 1787–89.

12 July 1789

Walking up a long hill, to ease my mare, I was joined by a poor woman who complained of the times and that it was a sad country; demanding her reasons, she said her husband had but a morsel of land, one cow, and a poor little horse, yet they had a franchar *[about 20 kg] of wheat and three chickens to pay ... to one* seigneur *and four* franchar *of oats, one chicken, and 1 sou to pay to another, besides very heavy* tailles *and other taxes. She had seven children, and the cow's milk helped to make the soup... It was said, at present, that something was to be done by some great folks for such poor ones, but she did not know who nor how, but God send us better, for we are being crushed by the tailles and dues. This woman, at no great distance might have been taken for sixty or seventy, her figure was so bent and her face so furrowed and hardened by labour – but she said she was only twenty-eight.*

Travels in France and Italy during the years 1787–89

The States General had been meeting since 5 May. See pages 16–17.

5 Which complaints in this extract confirm the complaints listed in the *cahier*?
6 What additional reasons does it provide to explain why life was hard for peasants and in particular for peasant women?

C These cartoons appeared in France in 1789 with the caption: 'it is to be hoped that this game will end soon'.

Questions
7 Who are the people being carried by the peasant man and woman? What is the artist suggesting by drawing the figures in this way? Choose two pieces of information from documents **A** and **B** which support this suggestion.
8 Consider the following questions in relation to documents **A**, **B** and **C**:
   a) Does it give us the views of one person or more than one?
   b) Does it give us the views of the peasants themselves?
   c) For what reason was it originally produced?
Now say which document you would attach most importance to as a source of information about peasant life at this time. Give reasons for your answer.

3

THE THREE ESTATES

France was traditionally divided into three groups or estates. The clergy made up the First Estate, the nobility was the Second Estate while the Third Estate consisted of everyone who was not a clergyman or a nobleman, i.e. the vast majority of the population.

A

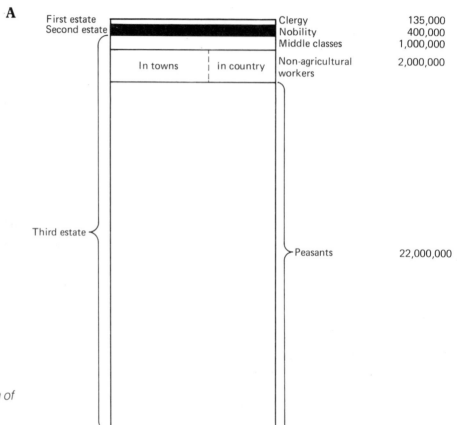

First estate	Clergy 135,000
Second estate	Nobility 400,000
	Middle classes 1,000,000
In towns ¦ in country	Non-agricultural workers 2,000,000
Third estate	Peasants 22,000,000

This diagram shows the number of people in each of the three estates in 1789

When the king summoned the States General each estate elected deputies or delegates to attend the proceedings. The number of delegates sent by each estate was as follows:

B First Estate (clergy)   300
Second Estate (nobility)   291
Third Estate (everyone else)   610
                              ─────
                              1 201

Every delegate had to wear the set uniform for their estate and obey numerous other regulations dating from when the States General had last met in 1614.

C

These were the uniforms for delegates representing the nobility, the Third Estate and the clergy

D   . . . it is not to be wondered at if the Third Estate was somewhat restive at regulations which instructed them to be attired in their customary suits of solemn black, to keep their hats off when the nobles and clergy followed the king in donning theirs, to be received by the king in a different manner and room from those prescribed for the first two Orders, and to enter the Assembly by a side door after the clergy and the nobility had walked in by the front.

Alfred Cobban: *A History of Modern France*, volume 1, 1957

Questions
1   Compare table **B** with the numbers of people in each estate given in diagram **A**. Which is the best-represented estate and which the least-well represented?
2   What conclusions do you draw from picture **C** and extract **D** about the king's attitude towards the Third Estate?

4

1789

The meeting of the States General

The long-awaited opening session of the States General was held on 5 May 1789. The 1 201 delegates, together with perhaps twice as many spectators, assembled in a huge hall in the palace at Versailles to await the arrival of the king. Some of them had a long wait. The representatives of the Third Estate were summoned for eight o'clock and the king did not appear until one o'clock. He opened the proceedings with a short speech and was followed first by the Lord Privy Seal, who could hardly be heard, and then by Jacques Necker, the Swiss banker now in charge of the country's finances. His detailed examination of the financial situation lasted for three hours (part of it was read by somebody else to save Necker's voice) and was very tedious.

The Third Estate delegates (who were mostly middle-class people such as lawyers and government officials) were disappointed and angry. There had been no mention of making France more democratic by giving some of the king's powers to an elected assembly. The king and his ministers clearly had no intention of making changes of this sort. If Louis expected the Third Estate deputies to accept this then he seriously misjudged their mood. One of them wrote on the evening of 5 May:

The States General, May 1789. Try to pick out the three groups of delegates

> *Let us hope that the Minister of Finance will understand, before it is too late, that the time for shilly-shallying is over; that it is no longer possible to resist the tide of public opinion – one must either swim with it, or be drowned.*

In order to change France the Third Estate deputies had first to win control of the States General. Once the opening ceremonies were over the three estates were to meet in separate chambers. Proposals would be passed if two of the chambers voted in favour. This would mean that the clergy and the nobility would be able to block any reforms proposed by the Third Estate, in spite of the fact that this group had more votes than the other two combined. For this reason the Third Estate argued that all representatives should meet in one hall and that decisions should be reached by a straightforward count of hands.

The revolt of the middle classes

In order to bring this about the Third Estate deputies asked the clergy and nobility to join them. Their request was ignored and so they decided to take the law into their own hands and proceed with their reforms. They had the right to do this, they argued, since they represented the whole nation except for the clergy and nobility (see page 14). To emphasise this they decided on 17 June to call themselves the National Assembly. Three days later, in the famous Tennis Court Oath, they expressed their determination to remain together until they had changed the way France was governed. When, on 23 June, the king ordered them to disperse, his messenger received this reply: '. . . we shall not leave: return to those who have sent you and tell them that we shall not stir from our places save at the point of the bayonet.' The king was bewildered by this show of defiance. Reluctantly he gave way and on 27 June agreed that the three estates should meet as one body. The Third Estate had won a great victory and the National Assembly, which after 9 July was known as the Constituent Assembly, was ready to begin the job of reform.

The Tennis Court Oath, 20 June 1789, as painted by David, the Revolution's most famous painter. The person circled is Maximilien de Robespierre (see pages 41–2)

The storming of the Bastille

At this stage violence erupted in Paris. News of troops being assembled near the city led to rumours that the king intended to dismiss the Constituent Assembly and was prepared to use force if necessary. Fear and anger swept through the capital. Street orators urged people to arm themselves and to be prepared to fight for reform, and soon crowds were surging everywhere seeking weapons.

On 14 July a crowd surrounded the Bastille. This was a prison but it was also a royal fortress where many weapons were stored. Its outer defences were weak and the mob soon occupied the surrounding courts. At this point 300 mutinous troops arrived and trained five cannon on the main drawbridge and gate. For two hours these guns pounded the fortress until Governor de Launey decided to surrender. The victorious mob was soon parading his head on a pike. Several

The storming of the Bastille,
14 July 1789

other defenders were killed and the rest were hustled off to prison.
One survivor wrote:

> *The streets through which we passed and the houses flanking them*
> *(even the roof-tops) were filled with masses of people insulting and*
> *cursing me. Swords, bayonets and pistols were being continually*
> *pressed against me. I did not know how I should die but felt that my*
> *last moment had come. Those who had no arms threw stones at me*
> *and the women gnashed their teeth at me and threatened me with their*
> *fists.*

Following the fall of the Bastille the offending troops were moved
from around Paris. Once again Louis had been forced to give way.
Three days later he visited Paris and accepted the tricolour as France's
new national flag. It was significant that the three colours were the red
and blue of Paris with the royal white in between.

When the Bastille was taken only seven prisoners could be found in
its dungeons. Nevertheless the event seemed to mark the dawn of a
new age. For years the word 'Bastille' had struck terror into people's
hearts. Now they had seized it. Clearly the king's authority was
crumbling and momentous changes were in the air.

The revolt of the peasants

The events of 14 July were part of a wave of violence which swept the country during the summer months of 1789.

The summoning of the States General had led the peasants to expect changes. They had been asked to state their grievances in the *cahiers*. This they had done and ever since 5 May they had been expecting action. In particular many peasant landowners had hoped that the States General would abolish feudal dues. So far they had waited in vain and now, spurred on by hunger, they decided to take action themselves. They attacked *seigneurs'* homes throughout much of France and destroyed the official documents listing the dues they were supposed to pay. Alarmed by this the Count of Germiny sent the following complaint to the Constituent Assembly:

> ... *On 29 July 1789 a group of brigands from elsewhere, together with my vassals and those of Vrighi, the next parish to mine, two hundred in all, came to my* château *at Sassy ... and, after breaking the locks on the cupboards containing my title deeds, they seized the registers which could be so necessary to me and took them away, or burned them in the woods, near my* château; *my guard was unable to offer any resistance ...*

vassals: those within his area of influence as *seigneur*
château: castle

A rumour went round that noblemen were employing bands of brigands to restore order, and this made the peasants angrier and more violent. With the countryside in chaos there was little the Assembly could do except to give way to the peasants' demands and abolish the feudal dues (4–11 August).

Having got what they wanted the peasants now returned to their work. For them the Revolution was over.

Assignment
1789: a summary of events
Below is a jumbled-up list of some of the events you have been reading about. Working in pairs, and without using the book, first put the events in the order in which they happened. Then look up the dates and so complete the date chart.

Date	Event
	Taking of the Bastille Abolition of feudal dues Opening session of the States General Louis agrees to the three estates meeting together Tennis Court Oath Third Estate calls itself the National Assembly

The impact of bread shortages

A *Price of 4 lb (1.8 kg) loaf in Paris*

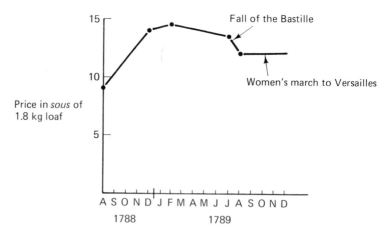

B *Percentage of income spent on bread by Parisian workers in 1789*

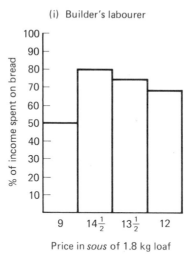

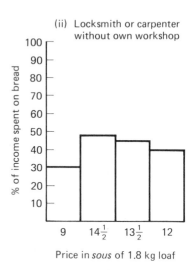

C *The woman had both to procure the food and to cook it; all her husband had to do was eat what she prepared and judge whether he was hungry or not. What she got was often the result of hours of waiting. She stood in the endless queues, each one a hotbed of discontent, hoping that when her turn came something would be left...*

D *... it was easier for a father to opt out than for a mother to do so – easier for him to return home via the cabaret suitably anaesthetised with cheap alcohol to the squalor of home and hungry children and easier for him as well to clear off altogether...*

cabaret: bar
anaesthetised: numbed

Source for **C** and **D**: Olwen Hufton
Women in Revolution 1789–1796
(*Past & Present* no. 53, November 1971)

1 What do B(i) & (ii) tell us about the effect on Paris workers of the price increases shown in graph A? What do they suggest about the diet of these people?
2 How useful would graph A be without tables B(i) and (ii) as a source of information about how Parisians lived in 1789?
3 Why, according to extract C, were women likely to be aware before men of the extent of food shortages?
4 What reasons are given in extract D to explain why the man of the house might resort to drink? What additional problems would this create for his wife?
5 Suggest why it was easier for the man to disappear than for the woman. How would his disappearance affect the abandoned wife?
6 Women usually played a leading part in bread riots. In what ways do extracts C and D help to explain this?

A tailor measures his wealthy client for some new clothes while her maidservant looks on. The extravagant way of life of the wealthy created jobs for many people

faubourgs: suburbs

Sound the tocsin! The march to Versailles, 5–6 October 1789

Throughout the Revolution there were days, like 14 July, when the people of Paris took to the streets, resorted to violence and in so doing dramatically altered the course of events. This happened in October 1789 when the women of Paris marched to Versailles in order to bring the king to the capital.

The summer of 1789 was a time of almost continuous unrest in Paris. There were various reasons for this. Unemployment was on the increase, especially amongst those who had worked for the nobility, many of whom were now fleeing the country. Wig-makers, tailors and domestic servants all suffered, as did seamstresses, milliners, corset-makers and the other garment trades. Many of the newly unemployed were, therefore, women at a time when the wife's wage played a vital part in the survival of many families. The most important reason for distress was, however, the scarcity of food. The 1788 harvest had been disastrous, and although that of 1789 was good, a drought in August prevented millers from using their water mills to grind their corn. As a result the price of bread remained high, bread-queues lengthened and mounting tension erupted into violence. Bailly, Mayor of Paris since 15 July, wrote in August that:

The cartloads of flour in our convoys are not only pillaged on the way by mobs, but are also pillaged in Paris by bakers who wait for them in the faubourgs *... such disorder creates two serious problems; the first is that the distribution of flour is unequal: one baker has too much, another not enough; the second is that the Paris Market is poorly stocked, which disturbs public opinion.*

As always in times of food shortage people suspected a conspiracy. Bakers were accused of hoarding, as were the city authorities. Protest demonstrations were held, and for sixteen days in September things were so bad that guards had to be posted in bakers' shops. In the bread queues feelings ran high and women were often the losers as they were roughly pushed to one side by men wanting a place at the front of the queue. By now women were playing a leading part in the agitation. To prevent suspected hoarding by bakers, they seized grain carts coming into the city and handed them over to the city authorities. Then on 17 September Mayor Bailly was forced to hear the angry complaints of a crowd of women who had surrounded the Town Hall.

The journalists and street orators, who had been demanding for some weeks that the king should no longer live at his palace at Versailles, used this state of affairs to their own advantage. Louis had refused to approve two measures passed by the Constituent Assembly. These were the Declaration of the Rights of Man (see page 25) and the August decrees abolishing feudal dues (see page 26). His refusal was condemned in the streets of Paris as clear evidence of the dangerous influence of those who surrounded him at Versailles. Suspicions were further aroused when the king summoned extra troops to Versailles.

Women on the march to Versailles, 5 October 1789

22

What seems finally to have driven the women of Paris to act was news of a banquet held for these troops on 2 October. At this banquet drunken soldiers had denounced the Revolution and declared their unswerving loyalty to the king and queen. In Paris the incident was angrily condemned in newspapers and at meetings; then on 5 October, a wet, miserable day, the tocsin sounded and the women began to march.

tocsin: signal for action provided by the church bells

Most were hungry and many were armed. Not all were poor. A few were smartly dressed and clearly well-to-do. Some men went with them and they were followed by 20 000 National Guards under the command of Lafayette who had been ordered by the municipal government of Paris to return with the king. Ahead lay a six-hour walk along heavily wooded roads which were notorious as the haunt of murderous robbers. On this occasion there was safety in numbers. The first women reached Versailles in the late afternoon. Louis was out hunting but when he returned to find a huge crowd outside the palace he agreed to receive a deputation of six women. Alarmed by the turn of events he promised extra supplies of bread and approved the August decrees and the Declaration of the Rights of Man. He had no intention, however, of returning to Paris.

At dawn the next day some of the crowd found a way into the palace and made for the queen's rooms. They killed two of the palace guards, and Marie-Antoinette had to flee to safety. The National Guard restored order but the mood of the crowd remained angry. When the royal family appeared later on the palace balcony the cry went up: 'to Paris'. A few hours later the women of Paris were triumphantly escorting the royal carriage containing the king and queen back to the capital.

Louis never returned to Versailles. The members of the Constituent Assembly followed him ten days later and thereafter the main action of the Revolution took place in Paris.

To Versailles!

Assignment

You are one of the Parisians marching to Versailles. As you walk you talk with those around you about why you are going to Versailles. Describe:
a) how you and your family have been affected by unemployment and shortages of food,
b) how you heard the news of troops being moved to Versailles and of events at the banquet which followed,
c) how you felt about these pieces of news and why you were prepared to march to Versailles,
d) what you intend to do when you get there.

5 LIBERTY

The French Revolution was, among other things, about ideas — ideas which excited and inspired:

> *Bliss was it in that dawn to be alive,*
> *But to be young was very heaven!*

So wrote the poet Wordsworth of his time in France during the early years of the Revolution. Some of the main ideas of the Revolution were summed up in the phrase 'Liberty, Equality, Fraternity'. This became the slogan of the Revolution, challenging the old order and offering to replace it with something better. What exactly did it mean? In this chapter we shall look at the word 'Liberty'.

The changes made by the Constituent Assembly help to explain this painting of the French frontier by Goethe. The sign reads: 'Travellers, this land is free'

A A starting point might be the way we use the word today:

> liberty: *the power or right to do as one chooses: 'our parents allowed us total* liberty *at an early age'.*
>
> Heinemann English Dictionary

B We can also look at the Declaration of Rights passed by the Constituent Assembly on 26 August 1789. The ideas of liberty and equality lie very much at the heart of this document. The ideas in the Declaration were not new. Educated French people had been discussing many of them for decades. What was new was the way the Declaration drew together ideas which had been developing over a long period of time and made them into a plan for future action. The Declaration had seventeen articles. Here are two of them:

> (iv) *Liberty consists in being able to do whatever does not harm others.*
>
> (xi) *The free communication of thought and opinion is one of the most precious rights of man: every citizen can therefore talk, write and publish freely.*

C The deputies in the Constituent Assembly put these ideas into practice over the next two years. The changes they made are summarised on pages 26–7.

Group assignments

In each case groups should report on their findings to the rest of the class.

1 For 'liberty' we sometimes use the word 'freedom'. Discuss what you think are important ways in which you are free. After writing them down, mark the six most important freedoms for your group and give your reasons for choosing them.

2 Read article (iv) in the Declaration. Write down the things you are not free to do if liberty is defined in this way. Start with those actions which would cause most harm to others and finish with the least harmful. Give reasons for the order you choose.

3 Read pages 26–7. Choose two of these changes and explain how they gave people in France more freedom.

1789~91

The work of the Constituent Assembly

The Constituent Assembly tried to put into practice the ideas set out in the Declaration of Rights (see pages 24–5). As a result there were more important changes during the years 1789–91 than at any other time during the Revolution. Here are some of them:

1789
Abolition of feudal dues including tithes. Abolition of torture and hanging. The old noble privilege of being executed by the sword was now extended to everyone. The guillotine was introduced in 1792 as a humane way of carrying this out.
Confiscation of all Church property. The sale of these lands, about a tenth of France, together with the issue of a new paper currency, the

A cartoon showing (left) *a wealthy clergyman before the Revolution and* (right) *his changed situation after the events of 1789*

assignats, helped to solve, for the time being, the country's financial problems.

Reorganisation of local government. The old administrative areas disappeared and France was divided into eighty-three departments which were subdivided into districts and then communes. All officials were to be elected.

1790

Abolition of all noble titles. Reform of the legal system. Trial by jury was introduced in criminal cases as was the right of an arrested person to be released after twenty-four hours if there was no case against him. Judges were to be elected.

Civil Constitution of the Clergy. All clergy were to be elected by their congregations. They would be paid by the government as the Church had now lost its wealth. Later the Assembly ordered all clergy to swear their loyalty to these changes. Many clergy saw this as conflicting with their first loyalty to the Catholic Church and to God and refused. Later, a great deal of opposition to the Revolution was to centre round these 'non-juring' or 'non-swearing' priests.

1791

Constitution. As its name suggests, the main job of the Constituent Assembly was to draw up a new constitution or system of government. This was finally approved in September 1791 and very much reduced the king's powers. In future new laws would have to be approved by a Legislative Assembly elected by so-called 'active' (as opposed to 'passive') citizens. These were men who paid direct taxes equal to a labourer's wages for three days. About 4 000 000 men qualified for the vote and they would also elect judges, priests and local government officials.

A print of 1791 showing the three estates hammering out the new constitution together

EQUALITY

As we have seen, the leaders of the French Revolution laid great stress on the idea of 'equality'.

A   *From* The Declaration of the Rights of Man and the Citizen, *1789*
  (i)   *Men are born and remain free and equal in rights.*
  (ii) *These rights are liberty, [the right to own] property, security and resistance to oppression.*
  (vi) *The law should express the will of the people. All citizens have the right to take part personally, or through their representatives, in the making of the Law. It should be the same for everyone, whether it protects or punishes. Jobs and honours are to be open to all citizens who will be selected only on the basis of ability.*

B   By reading pages 26–7 you can see how the Constituent Assembly put these ideas into practice.

Group assignments
1   Discuss the ways in which you are equal with each other. Write them down and mark the six most important equalities for your group. Give reasons for your choice.
2   It is sometimes important to spot what has not been said. Read extract **A**. If these ideas were put into practice can you think of any ways in which people would remain unequal?
3   Article (vi) of the Declaration says that the law should be the same for everyone. What evidence is there in the Restif story (page 7) to show that this was not the case before the Revolution?
4   Read pages 26–7. Choose two of these changes and explain how they made people in France more equal.
5   'All citizens have the right to take part personally, or through their representatives, in the making of the law.' How far was this idea put into practice in the Constitution of 1791 (page 27)?

---

8 THE OVERTHROW OF THE MONARCHY

The flight to Varennes, 20–21 June 1791

At 10.15 p.m. on Monday 20 June 1791 a hired carriage drew up at the back of the Tuileries, the royal palace in Paris where the king and queen had lived since being forced to leave Versailles in October 1789. For some time there had been rumours that the king intended to escape from Paris, and so guards had been posted round the palace. One door, however, had been left unguarded; the royal children slipped out of it, the Dauphin disguised as a girl and their governess posing as their wealthy Russian mother. The carriage disappeared and returned about three-quarters of an hour later to pick up a 'nursery maid', a 'valet' and a 'governess' called Madame Rocher. These three were in fact the king's sister, the king and Queen Marie-Antoinette.

Clattering through the quiet streets the carriage made for the Saint-Martin customs post to the north of the city, where a large travelling coach was waiting. The party transferred into this and at 1.30 a.m. set off for Châlons, about 160 kilometres from Paris.

Dauphin: heir to the throne

Queen Marie-Antoinette in 1791

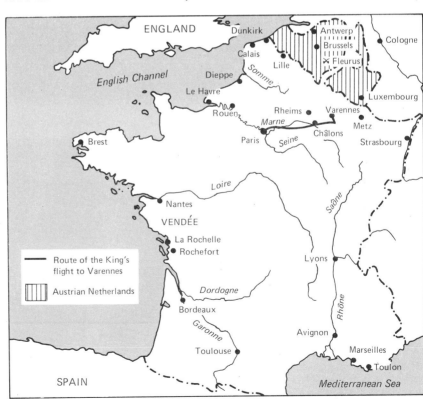

France in 1789

The plan was to make for Montmédy, near the frontier with the Austrian Netherlands. The road passed through the forest of the Argonne which, like the other woodlands around Paris, was the home of numerous bandit groups only too ready to set upon travellers. At the post-houses along the route fresh horses were waiting for the royal coach, and at various points beyond Châlons detachments of cavalry were waiting to provide an escort. Once at Montmédy the king intended to declare his opposition to the Revolution and his determination to recover his powers. He hoped for support from his brother-in-law, the Austrian Emperor, and was prepared if necessary to make use of Austrian troops.

The carefully laid plans did not work out. The journey to Châlons took longer than expected. The coach could only manage eleven kilometres an hour, and problems with a harness caused delay. As a result the commander of the first detachment of waiting cavalry decided to withdraw his men and sent a message along the route to the frontier saying that the royal coach would not be coming that day. There was, therefore, no escort. At Châlons the king was recognised, and again a few miles further on at Sainte-Ménehould. The postmaster here realised who the valet was from the image of the king's face on the *assignats* he had been paid for the horses. He raised the alarm and, together with a companion, went after the coach. By riding across country they reached Varennes before the coach and arranged for the inhabitants to block the road. Some time between eleven and twelve o'clock at night the travellers were duly forced to dismount, and the king admitted who he was; by 7.30 a.m. the next day the royal coach party, now with an escort of National Guards, was on its way back to Paris.

The inhabitants of Varennes halt the royal coach during the night of 21/22 June 1791

Question
The royal plan of escape failed. Can you suggest some changes to the plan which might have made it successful?

Results of the flight

The journey to Paris took three and a half days and provided ample evidence of the mood of the people. Hostile crowds hurled abuse at the passing royal coach. They felt betrayed. It was now clear for all to see that the king disapproved of the Revolution. Back in Paris the Constituent Assembly had to decide what to do. Many Parisians wanted Louis to abdicate. Six thousand of them signed a petition demanding this on 17 July. Yet the Assembly had now virtually completed the Constitution which provided for Louis to remain king but with far less power than before the Revolution. It decided to ignore popular feeling and to press ahead with the Constitution. The king publicly accepted the new Constitution on 14 September 1791. However, few now believed that he intended to abide by it, and people were right to be suspicious. Only six days before, the queen had secretly written to her brother, the Austrian Emperor, pleading with him for help. The letter started:

To put an end to the troubles of the French Revolution depends on the Emperor. There is no longer any possibility of conciliation.

Armed force has destroyed everything; only armed force can repair the damage.

A critic of the Constitution of 1791

The king and his supporters disliked the Constitution because it was too democratic. Most others disliked it because it was not democratic enough. Maximilien de Robespierre was one of these. Here is part of a speech by him published in April 1791. He was a member of the Assembly who belonged to the Jacobin Club, one of numerous political clubs in existence at this time:

Is the law the expression of the will of the people when the greater number of those for whom it is made can have no hand whatever in its making? No.

Question

Which part of the Constitution is Robespierre criticising and for what reason?

The sans-culottes

The Constitution of 1791 was intended to mark the end of the Revolution, but within a year it had been abandoned as a result of the great uprising of 10 August 1792 in which 1 200 people died. One reason it did not last was that many Parisians agreed with Robespierre's criticisms. This was especially the case among the *sans-culottes*.

The *sans-culottes* were, in the main, the craftsmen and traders of Paris, and they made up the bulk of the city's population, as they did in other towns. They included shoemakers and tailors, shopkeepers and publicans. Some were clerks; others were, or had been, professional soldiers. Some were employers; others were employees. A few were rich; most were poor enough to be worried about the price of food. In some ways they were a varied collection of people, but they were united in their enthusiasm for the Revolution. They despised the old nobility and refused to wear breeches, or *culottes*, as these had been an aristocratic fashion. Instead they wore trousers (hence their name: 'without breeches'). One of their number, a professional soldier called Vingterguier, wrote the following description of a typical *sans-culotte* in 1793:

A   *A* sans-culottes, *you rogues? He is someone who always goes about on foot, who has not got the millions you would all like to have, who has no* châteaux, *no servants to wait on him, and who lives simply with his wife and children, if he has any, on the fourth or fifth storey. He is useful because he knows how to till a field, to forge iron, to use a saw, to roof a house, to make shoes, and to spill his blood to the last drop for the safety of the Republic. And because he is a worker, you are sure not to meet his person in the Café de Chartres, or in the gaming houses where others plot and wager, nor in the National Theatre . . .*

In the evening he goes to the assembly of his Section; not powdered and perfumed and nattily booted, in the hope of being noticed by the citizenesses in the galleries, but ready to support sound proposals with all his might and ready to pulverise those which come from the despised faction of politicians.

Finally, a sans-culotte *always has his sabre well-sharpened, ready to cut off the ears of all opponents of the Revolution . . .*

Quoted in D. G. Wright: *Revolution and Terror in France 1789–1795,* 1974

Section: in 1790 Paris was divided into forty-eight sections, each with its elected assembly

B   The following prints of a *sans-culotte* man and woman appeared in England in 1794:

Questions

1 Read passage **A**. What evidence is there in this passage that the *sans-culotte* prided himself on being a hard worker?
2 Why does the writer disapprove of gaming houses? Can you suggest any other reasons why *sans-culottes* should disapprove of gambling and other similar activities?
3 Meetings of the locally elected assemblies were very well attended at this time. What two contrasting explanations of this are suggested by this passage?
4 Do you think this description of a typical *sans-culotte* is likely to be completely accurate? Give reasons for your answer.
5 Study pictures **B**(i) and (ii). What kind of people were the *sans-culottes* according to this artist?
6 Why do you think the artist has drawn the *sans-culottes* in this way? Bear in mind that England and France were at war from 1793 onwards.

War!

On 20 April 1792 France declared war on Austria. In May Austria was joined by her ally Prussia. So began a war which was to last more or less continuously until 1815 and was to involve, at one time or another, virtually every country in Europe.

The war sealed Louis' fate. Many of his strongest opponents had wanted war because they felt it would force him to show his true

Europe in 1789

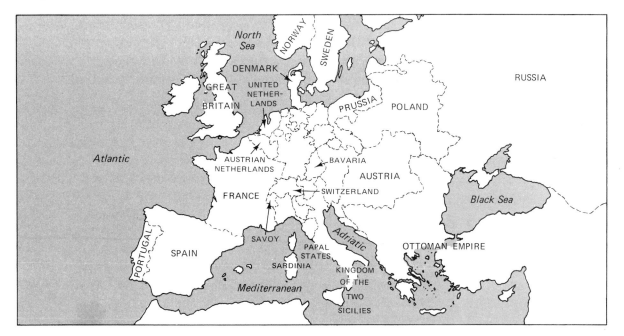

colours as someone working alongside the enemies of France. When this happened, they calculated, the people would dethrone him and France would become a republic (a country without a monarch). Certainly Louis and his supporters hoped for a swift Austrian victory and worked to bring this about. On the eve of the outbreak of war, Marie-Antoinette wrote to the Austrian ambassador with details of the French plan of attack. 'It is well to know this plan,' she wrote, 'so we can be on our guard and take all necessary measures.' She continued her secret correspondence with her brother throughout the summer.

Rumours soon began to circulate about the 'Austrian Committee' at the Tuileries and people became more suspicious when news reached the capital of defeats on the battlefield. The French army lacked experienced officers because of the mass emigration of the nobility since 1789. The troops were undisciplined and badly equipped. Their hopes of an easy conquest of the Austrian Netherlands were quickly dashed and before long they were in retreat. The Austrian and Prussian forces led by the Duke of Brunswick pushed, somewhat slowly, towards Paris and panic swept through the capital. Emergency measures were taken. Twenty thousand National Guards were summoned from the provinces to replace regular troops normally garrisoned in Paris but now needed on the frontier. These *fédérés*, as they were called, included a contingent from Marseilles who entered Paris on 30 July singing their stirring battle song, now France's national anthem, *la Marseillaise*. On 11 July the Assembly declared 'the fatherland' to be in danger, and called on all Frenchmen capable of using a weapon to rally to its defence. Three weeks later it decreed that every Frenchman was to be given a pike.

This was the situation when news reached Paris of a document apparently written by the enemy commander, the Duke of Brunswick, on 25 July and known ever since as the Brunswick Manifesto. It spoke on behalf of the Austrian Emperor and the King of Prussia, and included the following warning to the people of Paris:

> ... *if the Palace of the Tuileries is entered by force or attacked, if the least violence, the least outrage be done Their Majesties the King, the Queen and the Royal Family, if their security, preservation, and liberty be not provided for immediately, they will exact an exemplary and ever-memorable vengeance thereon by delivering the city of Paris to military punishment and total destruction, and the rebels who are guilty of outrages, to the punishments they deserve.*

The Marseillaise

the King: i.e. Louis XVI

Question

Bearing in mind the rumours already circulating about the royal family, what conclusions do you think the people of Paris were likely to draw from the Brunswick Manifesto?

10 August 1792

If the Brunswick Manifesto was intended to safeguard Louis and his family, it had exactly the opposite effect. The *sans-culottes* were now determined to act. On the morning of 10 August an angry crowd of about 20 000 *sans-culottes* and *fédérés* marched on the Tuileries. Fighting broke out and the royal family fled for protection to the Legislative Assembly. The palace was set on fire and 600 of the Swiss guards defending it were killed. The following account by one of the attackers gives some idea of the savagery of the day's events:

The Swiss were cut to pieces. Some were killed in the state-rooms, others in the garden. Many died on the Champs-Elysées. Heavens! That Liberty should cost Frenchmen blood and tears! How many victims there were among both the People and the National Guard! The total number of dead could run to 2000. All the Swiss who had been taken prisoner were escorted to the Place de Grève. There they had their brains blown out. They were traitors sacrificed to vengeance. What vengeance! I shivered to the roots of my being. At least 47 heads were cut off. The Grève was littered with corpses, and heads were paraded on the ends of several pikes.

10 August 1792

The September Massacres, 1792. The war against Austria and Prussia was not going well at this time and a rumour spread that royalists imprisoned in Paris intended to break out of prison and join forces with the invaders. Paris workers attacked the prisons and brutally murdered between 1 100 and 1 400 prisoners

A sketch by David of Marie-Antoinette on her way to execution

Long live the Republic!

The *sans-culottes* wanted both the monarchy and the Legislative Assembly to go. After such a terrifying outburst of violence the Legislative Assembly was in no mood to refuse their demands. Louis was immediately suspended from office and placed under guard. The Legislative Assembly was to be replaced by a National Assembly or Convention elected by all Frenchmen and this would decide the long-term fate of the monarchy.

The Convention met for the first time on 20 September 1792. The next day it dethroned Louis and declared France a republic. To emphasise the break with the past it also decreed that the year should be changed and that 22 September 1792 was to mark the beginning of year one of the republic.

In November an iron chest was discovered at the Tuileries which contained details of the royal correspondence with the Austrians. Suspicions were now confirmed. Louis was tried for treason by the Convention, found guilty and, on 21 January 1793, executed (see pages 5–6). Marie-Antoinette followed him to the scaffold on 16 October of the same year.

9 FRATERNITY

By 1791 liberty and equality had been joined by a third idea, fraternity, and so the famous slogan of 'Liberty, Equality, Fraternity' was born. Fraternity means brotherhood, and the Revolutionary leaders wanted to convey their belief in the brotherhood of peoples, whatever their language or background. Having won liberty and equality for themselves it was now the duty of the French people to spread these ideas throughout Europe. This would be done by a war, not of conquest but of liberation.

This inspiration to spread the Revolution throughout Europe was an important reason behind France declaring war on Austria in April 1792 (see pages 33–4).

A   *The National Assembly declares that the French nation will refuse to undertake any war of conquest, and will never employ its forces against the liberty of any people.*

Decree, 29 December 1791

B   *The National Convention declares, in the name of the French people, that it will give fraternity and assistance to all peoples who shall wish to recover their liberty . . . The present decree shall be translated and printed in all languages.*

Decree, 19 November 1792

C

Group assignments

1   Discuss the things you have in common with one another, for example your age, where you live, your likes and dislikes. Write them down (leaving aside physical characteristics) and mark the three most important for your group. Give reasons for your choice.
2   Imagine situations which might arise in which you would feel a sense of fraternity and would help each other. Give three examples. In each case state the problem and then describe how people in the group would help.
3   Television provides one way of finding out what we have in common with people in other countries. List at least three programmes which have either been shown in other countries or are documentaries about them. What common interests do these indicate?
4   This appeal for help appeared in 1982.

LEBANON EMERGENCY

We see daily reports of the fighting and loss of lives in the Lebanon, but little is said about the survivors

Oxfam is desperately in need of funds to help with reconstruction and distribution of food, medical supplies and blankets.

List other cases you can think of where one country has urgently needed, and received, help from other countries.

5   Read extract **B**. The French clearly felt they were helping other peoples to improve their lives. List six changes that took place as a result of the Revolution which a French person might recommend to people in other countries.
6   Study picture **C**. Who is the figure on the left and what is he causing to happen? Write an appropriate caption.

THE REIGN OF TERROR, 1793~4

A Parisian's return

In the following passage the writer is returning to Paris after an absence of ten months. He used to live in the capital, but since 1789 has spent most of his time in the provinces, away from the Terror:

We reached the terminus, I got down, taking under my arm a packet containing a few articles of clothing which I needed and I was leaving the coaching office for the home of a friend from whom I intended to beg for hospitality. At the door of the office there was a sort of sentry who took my packet away from me on the ground that I was not allowed to carry anything at night. He told me I could come and call for it next day at the guard room. I withdrew without making any remark and proceeded to the house of my friend who had heard nothing of me for a year and a half and who, having turned Jacobin in the interval as a form of insurance, thought more about his own safety than about the fate of his former friends.

It was nearly nine o'clock when I knocked at his door. This would not have been thought unduly late in normal times, but as it was, my knocking at the door at such an hour caused a panic among all the people who lived in the house ... most of the crowd of citizens who thronged the prisons had been arrested after dark. The sound of a hammer caused every hearer to tremble, and my former friend seemed to be particularly alarmed when he saw me come into his house. Without asking after my health or enquiring what had happened to me and why I had come to Paris, he gave me to understand in curt, clear language, that as I had left Paris some time back it would be dangerous for me to stay in the city and for him to offer me shelter. 'What? It would be dangerous for me to stay the night?' I asked. 'Yes, it would,' he replied. 'If they came now to search the place, I should be a lost man.'

Questions
1 What evidence is there in this passage that the number of people being arrested at this time was very high?
2 The writer says that his friend had turned Jacobin 'as a form of insurance'. What conclusions do you draw from this?
3 Why should the fact that the writer had left Paris make him a dangerous man to put up for the night?

The famous Parisian 'knitting-women' watching an execution. A police report of 1793 commented: 'It is astonishing how ferocious women have become. Every day they are present at executions'

What was the Reign of Terror?

The Reign of Terror lasted from the summer of 1793 to the summer of 1794. As we have seen, this was a time when people lived in constant fear of arrest. Many of those arrested were guillotined. In Paris alone over 2 000 people were executed during this period. This was the time when tumbrils or wagons loaded with condemned prisoners rolled through the crowded streets of Paris while old hags sat waiting at the place of execution with their knitting. France was now governed by a small group of men who, together with their agents in the provinces, ruled literally by 'terror'. As a result many of the personal freedoms gained earlier in the Revolution (for example, an arrested person's right to a fair trial) now disappeared.

Why did the Terror take place?

The Reign of Terror came into being because of three separate crises which had developed by 1793, threatening to reduce France to chaos.

The foreign threat
Towards the end of 1792 the war against Austria and Prussia began to go well for France, and the Duke of Brunswick was forced to retreat to the frontier. In a fit of enthusiasm the Convention decided to extend the war, so that by March 1793 France was at war with most of Europe including Britain. Success soon turned to failure. A run of Austrian victories brought the enemy once more on to French soil and prompted the desertion of Dumouriez, a leading French general. France was again on the verge of complete defeat.

The threat at home
This was not the only military threat. In March 1793 a serious rebellion broke out in the Vendée, an area with plenty of hills and very few roads on the west coast of France. The rebellion was sparked off by the Convention's attempt to enforce conscription. The non-juring priests (see page 27) also played their part, as did those who wished to avenge the death of the king. Two months later there were the first rumblings of a whole series of revolts in the provinces in support of a political group called the Brissotins. The Brissotins (whose main support was in the provinces) held most of the important government jobs, but they were threatened by the Jacobins (who had the support of the Parisian *sans-culottes*). For months a bitter feud raged between the two groups. Then on 2 June 1793 a huge crowd of *sans-culottes* surrounded the Tuileries, where the Convention met, and demanded, successfully, the arrest of the leading Brissotins. This caused the provincial unrest to flare up. The Jacobins were now in power, but they faced Brissotin-inspired revolts in the north, centre and south of

France. There was unrest now in a total of sixty of the eighty-three departments of France.

Inflation

Matters were made worse by soaring inflation, caused by the over-issue of the currency of *assignats* (see page 27). Money therefore dropped in value, and by February 1793 it was worth only half the amount printed on it. Food was in short supply, as were other goods. The high price of soap, for example, was causing problems for the thousands of laundry women in Paris. As in the past, Parisians took the law into their own hands. They raided warehouses and shops and sold goods off at prices of their choosing. Concern about prices was a major reason why the *sans-culottes* wanted the Jacobins in power. They wanted tougher action against hoarders, who held on to stocks in the hope of selling when prices were higher, and also a more determined effort to hold down prices.

To cope with the increasingly desperate situation a special committee, the Committee of Public Safety, was elected by the Convention in April 1793. After the rising of 2 June, control of this Committee, and with it the whole of France, passed to the Jacobins. The Committee consisted of gifted but ruthless men who shared the tasks of government. The most widely known member was Robespierre.

Maximilien de Robespierre, 1758–94

Robespierre came from the provincial town of Arras. After being orphaned at the age of seven he lived with an uncle who sent him to school in Paris. He was a highly successful student and was chosen to read a speech of welcome to the king when Louis XVI visited the school. In 1781 he returned to Arras to work in the family legal practice. He worked hard and with some success, although the practice remained small. In his spare time he wrote verse and essays in which he made clear that he, like many other members of the middle classes, felt that France was ready for change (see page 17). It was fitting, therefore, that when the king summoned the States General in 1788 Robespierre should be elected as a delegate for Arras.

He was a strange-looking man, short and thin with a cat-like face. He dressed carefully, continued to powder his hair long after the fashion had gone out of practice and wore green-tinted glasses. He walked somewhat jerkily, periodically clenching his hands, and tended not to look people in the face when he spoke to them. By nature he was ambitious, and very much convinced that he was in the right. But he was lacking in a sense of humour, and had few close friends.

Robespierre held strong opinions and was not afraid to express them. Within a few months of the first meeting of the States General

Maximilien de Robespierre, 1758–94

in May 1789 he was well known, through his speeches in the Assembly and in the Jacobin Club, as a strong supporter of the Revolution. (Notice his prominent position in the painting of the Tennis Court Oath on page 17.) During the next two years he spoke up in favour of freedom of speech, against capital punishment and in favour of extending the vote to all adult males (see page 27). He championed the ordinary people of France, as in his speech of 11 August 1792:

> *Do you really think that a hard and laborious life produces more vices than luxury, ease, and ambition? Have you really less confidence in the virtue of our labourers and artisans ... than in that of tax-collectors, courtiers and the so-called nobility? ... in general there is no justice or goodness like that of the people.*

Small wonder he was by now one of the heroes of the Paris crowd.

Just over a year later, Robespierre was elected as one of the Convention's delegates for Paris. (All but one of the other twenty-three Parisian delegates were Jacobins.) His aim now was to get rid of the Brissotins, and he campaigned relentlessly against them. A month after they were overthrown he was elected to the Committee of Public Safety.

During the year in which he and his eleven colleagues ruled France, Robespierre never wavered in his commitment to the aims of the Revolution:

> *What is our aim? The quiet enjoyment of liberty and equality; the reign of that eternal justice whose laws are written, not on marble or stone, but in the heart of every man ...*

Equally he never doubted the need to rule by terror for, in his eyes, these great ideas of liberty and equality were now threatened by enemies at home and abroad:

> *Revolutionary government needs to be extraordinarily active, precisely because it is at war. It is subject to less uniform and rigorous rules, because the circumstances in which it finds itself are tempestuous and changing, and above all because it is obliged to employ ceaselessly new and urgent resources for new and pressing threats.*

Question

For Robespierre the aim of saving the Revolution justified the methods, whatever the cost in human terms. Do you think he was right? Give reasons for your answer.

The Reign of Terror

The threat at home

The Committee of Public Safety ordered the ruthless suppression of the countrywide revolts. The rebels were first defeated in battle and then punished. In Lyons nearly 2 000 rebels were shot and the houses of the rich systematically destroyed. In the Vendée, where resistance was strongest, Carrier, the Committee's *représentant en mission* (or agent) in Nantes, ordered mass drownings. On 23 December, for example, 800 prisoners ('of every age and sex' according to one witness) were drowned. The next day 300 more met the same fate and another 200 on Christmas Day.

By this time the revolts had collapsed, but the Committee remained afraid of any sign of opposition. Members of Jacobin clubs throughout the country were urged to report anybody whose loyalty they doubted. Under the Law of Suspects, passed in September 1793, a person could be arrested merely for lacking enthusiasm for the Revolution. One person was accused in Marseilles with the words: 'He possesses a very moderate patriotism.'

The accused were brought before special Revolutionary tribunals which worked swiftly and allowed no right of appeal. As the months passed, more of the accused were found guilty. During the 'great' Terror of June and July 1794 only one in five of those brought before the Revolutionary Tribunal in Paris was set free. The rest, 1 285 persons in all, were sent to the guillotine. Some of the condemned shouted warnings to the crowd from the scaffold: 'Citizens, beware lest you contaminate the soil of liberty with blood!' and again, 'It will be your turn next, perhaps tomorrow!'

The foreign threat

To deal with the foreign threat the Committee organised a massive war effort. The mass levy of August 1793 ordered everybody to play their part:

> *The young men will go to fight; married men will forge arms and transport food and supplies, women will make tents and uniforms and work in hospitals; children will find old rags for bandages; old men will appear in public places to excite the courage of warriors, the hatred of kings, and the unity of the Republic.*

This was a new way of waging war. It produced a huge army of 850 000 which was nearly three times as large as the combined enemy forces. To equip this army, church bells and railings were confiscated to provide metal, and government-run arms factories were established. J.M. Thompson describes the frantic efforts to produce guns.

> *Forges were set up everywhere; over two hundred and fifty could be counted in the squares, boulevards, and gardens of the capital.*

A *représentant en mission in the uniform designed by David the painter*

A cartoon attacking the Reign of Terror. The biggest pile of heads is labelled 'The People'. What is this suggesting about the Terror?

Convents were transformed into factories; cellars were scraped and dug for saltpetre; and thirty thousand pounds of gunpowder were produced every twenty-four hours from the great works at Grenelle.

The French Revolution, 1943

These measures worked. Towards the end of 1793 France's young generals, newly promoted from the ranks and spurred on by the example of unsuccessful colleagues who had been guillotined, led the French armies to a series of dramatic successes. In the following year victory at Fleurus on 26 June was followed by the re-occupation of the Austrian Netherlands.

Inflation

The Committee was less successful in its attempts to control prices. Food shortages led to serious unrest in Paris in September 1793 and as a result the General Maximum Law was passed. This fixed the prices of forty items, including food and drink, clothing and fuel. It also fixed wages, which annoyed the *sans-culottes*. At first the new law helped keep prices down, but goods remained in short supply and so prices soon began to rise again. Some shortages were created by the huge amounts of food consumed by the army, especially meat. Others resulted from hoarding, which remained widespread in spite of being punishable by death. Paris shopkeepers frequently had to buy their stock on the 'black market' at illegally high prices, and in spite of the General Maximum they passed these prices on to the customer. For example, in December 1793 butter in the Paris markets was selling at up to twice the official price.

A diagram comparing the old calendar (right) with the revolutionary calendar of September 1792. The new calendar changed the names of the months and introduced a ten day week. It was not popular. Can you suggest why?

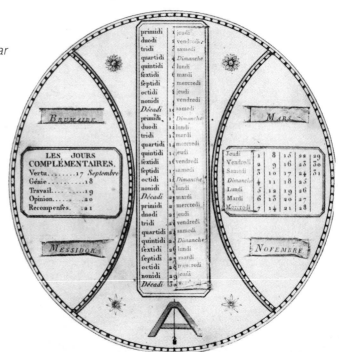

The end of the Terror

The *sans-culottes* were quick to point out that price controls were not working. In March 1794 one arms worker complained: 'We are more miserable than before because we can do nothing with our money and must die of hunger.' With prices continuing to rise, the *sans-culottes* resented bitterly the Committee's attempts to keep wages down. By the summer of 1794 various groups of workers, including arms workers, building workers and printers, were agitating for higher wages; some of them were prepared to defy the police and go on strike. The alliance between the *sans-culottes* and the Jacobins had clearly broken down, and for the Jacobins this was to prove fatal.

The Committee had been dramatically successful in dealing with the civil and foreign wars. In so doing it paved the way for its own downfall, because to the people there no longer seemed any need to rule by terror. On 27 July 1794 the delegates in the Convention, who felt threatened by Robespierre and his colleagues, found the courage to denounce them and vote their arrest. The *sans-culottes*, who might have kept the Committee in power, were in no mood to rally to its support. Robespierre's popularity with the Paris crowd had vanished and on 28 July he was guillotined along with twenty-one close supporters.

The Reign of Terror was over and so was the French Revolution.

During the Terror many churches were taken over as part of the dechristianising campaign

Complete the following summary chart of the Reign of Terror:

	Nature of the problem	Action taken by Committee of Public Safety	Results of this action
Foreign threat			
Threat at home			
Inflation			

The death of Marat, champion of the Terror

On 13 July 1793 Jean-Paul Marat, an outspoken supporter of the Terror and one of the great heroes of the *sans-culottes*, was murdered. His death brought a frenzied reaction from his supporters, and throughout the Reign of Terror he was worshipped as a martyr to the Revolutionary cause.

Marat was a doctor and scientist who became well known during the Revolution by writing a daily eight-page newspaper, *The Friend of the People*. His readers were the *sans-culottes* and he continually urged them to be ruthless in dealing with the enemies of the Revolution. This was his message when he became a Jacobin delegate in the Convention: 'Liberty must be established by violence . . .' he argued. His health was not good. He suffered from a painful skin disease and tried to ease the pain by taking frequent baths. He was in his bath when he was stabbed to death by Charlotte Corday, a supporter of the king.

A

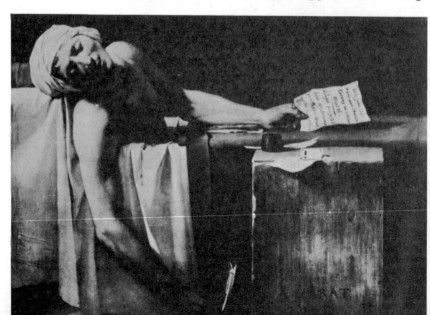

The assassination of Marat as painted by David (detail)

B *Marat's funeral*

The following report appeared in *The Times* on 18 July 1793:

> *The funeral of* Marat *was celebrated the day before yesterday, with the greatest pomp and solemnity... An immense crowd of people attended it. Four women bore the bathing-machine in which* Marat *was standing when he was assassinated; his shirt, stained with blood, was carried by another Amazon, at the top of a pike. After this followed a wooden bedstead, on which the corpse of* Marat *was carried by citizens. His head was uncovered, and the gash made by the knife of the assassin could be easily distinguished. The procession paraded through several streets, and was saluted on its march by several discharges of artillery.*

Amazon: powerfully built woman

C > *Instead of a monster whom people shunned,* Marat *became a martyr whom they worshipped. Plays, poems and hymns were written in his honour. Children were baptized Brutus-Marat, Sansculotte-Marat, and Marat-le-Montagne. Streets and Squares were called after him, and thirty-seven towns in different parts of France assumed his name.*
>
> J.M. Thompson: *Leaders of the French Revolution*, 1929

Questions

1 Study painting **A**. What kind of feelings do you think David was trying to arouse in those who saw the painting?

2 Had the camera been invented and a photograph been taken of the murder scene, how might it have differed from this painting?

3 Read extract **B**. On what points of detail does it appear to differ from the painting?

4 Why do you suppose the Jacobins a) ordered a funeral procession through the streets of Paris and b) included in that procession not only Marat's body but also his bath and bloodstained shirt?

5 Read extract **C**. Marat was more popular after his death than before. Can you suggest why this was so? Can you think of any other people who have become 'cult heroes' in this fashion?

Charlotte Corday on her way to the guillotine

INDEX